I0016389

The Personal

Internet

and Password Log

The Personal

Internet and Password Log

© Copyright 2018 Gary Wittmann

Reproduction or translation of any part of this work beyond that permitted by section 107 or 108 of the 1976 United States Copyright Act without permission of the copyright owner is unlawful. Requests for permission or further information should be addressed to the author.

This publication is designed to provide accurate and authoritative information in regard to the subject matter covered. It is sold the understanding that the publisher is not engaged in rendering legal, accounting, or other professional services. If legal advice or other expert assistance is required, the services of a competent professional person should be sought.

First Published, 2018

Printed in the United States of America

Website:

www.garywittmann.com

This an awesome journal that you can record <u>internet and computer information</u>.

The <u>password log</u> helps to record web address, username, password and notes.

At the beginning you will want to record <u>information about your provider and support.</u>

There is a great page for recording <u>personal contact</u> information.

This journal has four pages for writing <u>Birthdays</u> to remember.

It is with my love that this journal will keep you inform and a safe place to record valuable information.

The Monthly Blog page is for organizing your month and thoughts.

Useful Internet and Computer Information

Internet Provider Information

Account Number _____

Tech Support _____

Consumer Support _____

Telephone numbers: _____

Notes

_____

_____

_____

_____

_____

_____

Birthday calendar

January	February	March	April
_____	_____	_____	_____
_____	_____	_____	_____
_____	_____	_____	_____
_____	_____	_____	_____
_____	_____	_____	_____
_____	_____	_____	_____
_____	_____	_____	_____
_____	_____	_____	_____
_____	_____	_____	_____

May	June	July	August
_____	_____	_____	_____
_____	_____	_____	_____
_____	_____	_____	_____
_____	_____	_____	_____
_____	_____	_____	_____
_____	_____	_____	_____
_____	_____	_____	_____
_____	_____	_____	_____
_____	_____	_____	_____

September	October	November	December
_____	_____	_____	_____
_____	_____	_____	_____
_____	_____	_____	_____
_____	_____	_____	_____
_____	_____	_____	_____
_____	_____	_____	_____
_____	_____	_____	_____
_____	_____	_____	_____
_____	_____	_____	_____

Birthday calendar

January

February

March

April

May

June

July

August

September

October

November

December

Birthday calendar

January
_____
_____
_____
_____
_____
_____
_____
_____
_____
_____

February
_____
_____
_____
_____
_____
_____
_____
_____
_____
_____

March
_____
_____
_____
_____
_____
_____
_____
_____
_____
_____

April
_____
_____
_____
_____
_____
_____
_____
_____
_____
_____

May
_____
_____
_____
_____
_____
_____
_____
_____
_____
_____

June
_____
_____
_____
_____
_____
_____
_____
_____
_____
_____

July
_____
_____
_____
_____
_____
_____
_____
_____
_____
_____

August
_____
_____
_____
_____
_____
_____
_____
_____
_____
_____

September
_____
_____
_____
_____
_____
_____
_____
_____
_____
_____

October
_____
_____
_____
_____
_____
_____
_____
_____
_____
_____

November
_____
_____
_____
_____
_____
_____
_____
_____
_____
_____

December
_____
_____
_____
_____
_____
_____
_____
_____
_____
_____

Birthday calendar

January
_____
_____
_____
_____
_____
_____
_____
_____
_____

February
_____
_____
_____
_____
_____
_____
_____
_____
_____

March
_____
_____
_____
_____
_____
_____
_____
_____
_____

April
_____
_____
_____
_____
_____
_____
_____
_____
_____

May
_____
_____
_____
_____
_____
_____
_____
_____
_____

June
_____
_____
_____
_____
_____
_____
_____
_____
_____

July
_____
_____
_____
_____
_____
_____
_____
_____
_____

August
_____
_____
_____
_____
_____
_____
_____
_____
_____

September
_____
_____
_____
_____
_____
_____
_____
_____
_____

October
_____
_____
_____
_____
_____
_____
_____
_____
_____

November
_____
_____
_____
_____
_____
_____
_____
_____
_____

December
_____
_____
_____
_____
_____
_____
_____
_____
_____

Birthday calendar

January	February	March	April

May	June	July	August

September	October	November	December

Birthday calendar

January	February	March	April

May	June	July	August

September	October	November	December

Password Log

Web Address	Username	Password

Password Log

Web Address	Username	Password

Password Log

Web Address	Username	Password

Password Log

Web Address	Username	Password

Password Log

Web Address	Username	Password

Password Log

Web Address	Username	Password

Password Log

Web Address	Username	Password

Password Log

Web Address	Username	Password

Password Log

Web Address	Username	Password

Password Log

Web Address	Username	Password

Password Log

Web Address	Username	Password

Password Log

Web Address	Username	Password

Personal Contacts

Name & Address	Phone	Online	Special Dates
	Work: Home: Cell: Fax:	Email: Website: Facebook: Other:	Birthday: Anniversary:
	Work: Home: Cell: Fax:	Email: Website: Facebook: Other:	Birthday: Anniversary:
	Work: Home: Cell: Fax:	Email: Website: Facebook: Other:	Birthday: Anniversary:
	Work: Home: Cell: Fax:	Email: Website: Facebook: Other:	Birthday: Anniversary:
	Work: Home: Cell: Fax:	Email: Website: Facebook: Other:	Birthday: Anniversary:
	Work: Home: Cell: Fax:	Email: Website: Facebook: Other:	Birthday: Anniversary:
	Work: Home: Cell: Fax:	Email: Website: Facebook: Other:	Birthday: Anniversary:

Personal Contacts

Name & Address	Phone	Online	Special Dates
	Work: Home: Cell: Fax:	Email: Website: Facebook: Other:	Birthday: Anniversary:
	Work: Home: Cell: Fax:	Email: Website: Facebook: Other:	Birthday: Anniversary:
	Work: Home: Cell: Fax:	Email: Website: Facebook: Other:	Birthday: Anniversary:
	Work: Home: Cell: Fax:	Email: Website: Facebook: Other:	Birthday: Anniversary:
	Work: Home: Cell: Fax:	Email: Website: Facebook: Other:	Birthday: Anniversary:
	Work: Home: Cell: Fax:	Email: Website: Facebook: Other:	Birthday: Anniversary:
	Work: Home: Cell: Fax:	Email: Website: Facebook: Other:	Birthday: Anniversary:

Personal Contacts

Name & Address	Phone	Online	Special Dates
	Work:	Email:	Birthday:
	Home:	Website:	Anniversary:
	Cell:	Facebook:	
	Fax:	Other:	
	Work:	Email:	Birthday:
	Home:	Website:	Anniversary:
	Cell:	Facebook:	
	Fax:	Other:	
	Work:	Email:	Birthday:
	Home:	Website:	Anniversary:
	Cell:	Facebook:	
	Fax:	Other:	
	Work:	Email:	Birthday:
	Home:	Website:	Anniversary:
	Cell:	Facebook:	
	Fax:	Other:	
	Work:	Email:	Birthday:
	Home:	Website:	Anniversary:
	Cell:	Facebook:	
	Fax:	Other:	
	Work:	Email:	Birthday:
	Home:	Website:	Anniversary:
	Cell:	Facebook:	
	Fax:	Other:	
	Work:	Email:	Birthday:
	Home:	Website:	Anniversary:
	Cell:	Facebook:	
	Fax:	Other:	

Personal Contacts

Name & Address	Phone	Online	Special Dates
	Work: Home: Cell: Fax:	Email: Website: Facebook: Other:	Birthday: Anniversary:
	Work: Home: Cell: Fax:	Email: Website: Facebook: Other:	Birthday: Anniversary:
	Work: Home: Cell: Fax:	Email: Website: Facebook: Other:	Birthday: Anniversary:
	Work: Home: Cell: Fax:	Email: Website: Facebook: Other:	Birthday: Anniversary:
	Work: Home: Cell: Fax:	Email: Website: Facebook: Other:	Birthday: Anniversary:
	Work: Home: Cell: Fax:	Email: Website: Facebook: Other:	Birthday: Anniversary:
	Work: Home: Cell: Fax:	Email: Website: Facebook: Other:	Birthday: Anniversary:

Personal Contacts

Name & Address	Phone	Online	Special Dates
	Work: Home: Cell: Fax:	Email: Website: Facebook: Other:	Birthday: Anniversary:
	Work: Home: Cell: Fax:	Email: Website: Facebook: Other:	Birthday: Anniversary:
	Work: Home: Cell: Fax:	Email: Website: Facebook: Other:	Birthday: Anniversary:
	Work: Home: Cell: Fax:	Email: Website: Facebook: Other:	Birthday: Anniversary:
	Work: Home: Cell: Fax:	Email: Website: Facebook: Other:	Birthday: Anniversary:
	Work: Home: Cell: Fax:	Email: Website: Facebook: Other:	Birthday: Anniversary:
	Work: Home: Cell: Fax:	Email: Website: Facebook: Other:	Birthday: Anniversary:

Personal Contacts

Name & Address	Phone	Online	Special Dates
	Work: Home: Cell: Fax:	Email: Website: Facebook: Other:	Birthday: Anniversary:
	Work: Home: Cell: Fax:	Email: Website: Facebook: Other:	Birthday: Anniversary:
	Work: Home: Cell: Fax:	Email: Website: Facebook: Other:	Birthday: Anniversary:
	Work: Home: Cell: Fax:	Email: Website: Facebook: Other:	Birthday: Anniversary:
	Work: Home: Cell: Fax:	Email: Website: Facebook: Other:	Birthday: Anniversary:
	Work: Home: Cell: Fax:	Email: Website: Facebook: Other:	Birthday: Anniversary:
	Work: Home: Cell: Fax:	Email: Website: Facebook: Other:	Birthday: Anniversary:

Personal Contacts

Name & Address	Phone	Online	Special Dates
	Work: Home: Cell: Fax:	Email: Website: Facebook: Other:	Birthday: Anniversary:
	Work: Home: Cell: Fax:	Email: Website: Facebook: Other:	Birthday: Anniversary:
	Work: Home: Cell: Fax:	Email: Website: Facebook: Other:	Birthday: Anniversary:
	Work: Home: Cell: Fax:	Email: Website: Facebook: Other:	Birthday: Anniversary:
	Work: Home: Cell: Fax:	Email: Website: Facebook: Other:	Birthday: Anniversary:
	Work: Home: Cell: Fax:	Email: Website: Facebook: Other:	Birthday: Anniversary:
	Work: Home: Cell: Fax:	Email: Website: Facebook: Other:	Birthday: Anniversary:

Personal Contacts

Name & Address	Phone	Online	Special Dates
	Work:	Email:	Birthday:
	Home:	Website:	Anniversary:
	Cell:	Facebook:	
	Fax:	Other:	
	Work:	Email:	Birthday:
	Home:	Website:	Anniversary:
	Cell:	Facebook:	
	Fax:	Other:	
	Work:	Email:	Birthday:
	Home:	Website:	Anniversary:
	Cell:	Facebook:	
	Fax:	Other:	
	Work:	Email:	Birthday:
	Home:	Website:	Anniversary:
	Cell:	Facebook:	
	Fax:	Other:	
	Work:	Email:	Birthday:
	Home:	Website:	Anniversary:
	Cell:	Facebook:	
	Fax:	Other:	
	Work:	Email:	Birthday:
	Home:	Website:	Anniversary:
	Cell:	Facebook:	
	Fax:	Other:	
	Work:	Email:	Birthday:
	Home:	Website:	Anniversary:
	Cell:	Facebook:	
	Fax:	Other:	

Personal Contacts

Name & Address	Phone	Online	Special Dates
	Work:	Email:	Birthday:
	Home:	Website:	Anniversary:
	Cell:	Facebook:	
	Fax:	Other:	
	Work:	Email:	Birthday:
	Home:	Website:	Anniversary:
	Cell:	Facebook:	
	Fax:	Other:	
	Work:	Email:	Birthday:
	Home:	Website:	Anniversary:
	Cell:	Facebook:	
	Fax:	Other:	
	Work:	Email:	Birthday:
	Home:	Website:	Anniversary:
	Cell:	Facebook:	
	Fax:	Other:	
	Work:	Email:	Birthday:
	Home:	Website:	Anniversary:
	Cell:	Facebook:	
	Fax:	Other:	
	Work:	Email:	Birthday:
	Home:	Website:	Anniversary:
	Cell:	Facebook:	
	Fax:	Other:	
	Work:	Email:	Birthday:
	Home:	Website:	Anniversary:
	Cell:	Facebook:	
	Fax:	Other:	

Personal Contacts

Name & Address	Phone	Online	Special Dates
	Work: Home: Cell: Fax:	Email: Website: Facebook: Other:	Birthday: Anniversary:
	Work: Home: Cell: Fax:	Email: Website: Facebook: Other:	Birthday: Anniversary:
	Work: Home: Cell: Fax:	Email: Website: Facebook: Other:	Birthday: Anniversary:
	Work: Home: Cell: Fax:	Email: Website: Facebook: Other:	Birthday: Anniversary:
	Work: Home: Cell: Fax:	Email: Website: Facebook: Other:	Birthday: Anniversary:
	Work: Home: Cell: Fax:	Email: Website: Facebook: Other:	Birthday: Anniversary:
	Work: Home: Cell: Fax:	Email: Website: Facebook: Other:	Birthday: Anniversary:

Personal Contacts

Name & Address	Phone	Online	Special Dates
	Work: Home: Cell: Fax:	Email: Website: Facebook: Other:	Birthday: Anniversary:
	Work: Home: Cell: Fax:	Email: Website: Facebook: Other:	Birthday: Anniversary:
	Work: Home: Cell: Fax:	Email: Website: Facebook: Other:	Birthday: Anniversary:
	Work: Home: Cell: Fax:	Email: Website: Facebook: Other:	Birthday: Anniversary:
	Work: Home: Cell: Fax:	Email: Website: Facebook: Other:	Birthday: Anniversary:
	Work: Home: Cell: Fax:	Email: Website: Facebook: Other:	Birthday: Anniversary:
	Work: Home: Cell: Fax:	Email: Website: Facebook: Other:	Birthday: Anniversary:

Personal Contacts

Name & Address	Phone	Online	Special Dates
	Work: Home: Cell: Fax:	Email: Website: Facebook: Other:	Birthday: Anniversary:
	Work: Home: Cell: Fax:	Email: Website: Facebook: Other:	Birthday: Anniversary:
	Work: Home: Cell: Fax:	Email: Website: Facebook: Other:	Birthday: Anniversary:
	Work: Home: Cell: Fax:	Email: Website: Facebook: Other:	Birthday: Anniversary:
	Work: Home: Cell: Fax:	Email: Website: Facebook: Other:	Birthday: Anniversary:
	Work: Home: Cell: Fax:	Email: Website: Facebook: Other:	Birthday: Anniversary:
	Work: Home: Cell: Fax:	Email: Website: Facebook: Other:	Birthday: Anniversary:

Monthly Blog Stats

# Of Unique Visits:	
# Of Overall Visits:	
Total Page Views	
Total Posts Made	
Total Comments	
Top 3 Popular Posts	
Top 3 Incoming Traffic Sources	
Top 3 Keyword Searches	

Goals for Next Month:

Projects to Finish:

- ☐ _____
- ☐ _____
- ☐ _____
- ☐ _____
- ☐ _____
- ☐ _____
- ☐ _____
- ☐ _____
- ☐ _____
- ☐ _____

Projects to Start:

- ☐ _____
- ☐ _____
- ☐ _____
- ☐ _____
- ☐ _____
- ☐ _____
- ☐ _____
- ☐ _____
- ☐ _____
- ☐ _____

Monthly Blog Stats

# Of Unique Visits:	
# Of Overall Visits:	
Total Page Views	
Total Posts Made	
Total Comments	
Top 3 Popular Posts	
Top 3 Incoming Traffic Sources	
Top 3 Keyword Searches	

Goals for Next Month:

Projects to Finish:

- ☐ _____
- ☐ _____
- ☐ _____
- ☐ _____
- ☐ _____
- ☐ _____
- ☐ _____
- ☐ _____
- ☐ _____
- ☐ _____

Projects to Start:

- ☐ _____
- ☐ _____
- ☐ _____
- ☐ _____
- ☐ _____
- ☐ _____
- ☐ _____
- ☐ _____
- ☐ _____
- ☐ _____

Monthly Blog Stats

# Of Unique Visits:	
# Of Overall Visits:	
Total Page Views	
Total Posts Made	
Total Comments	
Top 3 Popular Posts	
Top 3 Incoming Traffic Sources	
Top 3 Keyword Searches	

Goals for Next Month:

Projects to Finish:

- ☐ _____
- ☐ _____
- ☐ _____
- ☐ _____
- ☐ _____
- ☐ _____
- ☐ _____
- ☐ _____
- ☐ _____
- ☐ _____

Projects to Start:

- ☐ _____
- ☐ _____
- ☐ _____
- ☐ _____
- ☐ _____
- ☐ _____
- ☐ _____
- ☐ _____
- ☐ _____
- ☐ _____

Monthly Blog Stats

# Of Unique Visits:	
# Of Overall Visits:	
Total Page Views	
Total Posts Made	
Total Comments	
Top 3 Popular Posts	
Top 3 Incoming Traffic Sources	
Top 3 Keyword *Searches	

Goals for Next Month:

Projects to Finish:

☐ _____
☐ _____
☐ _____
☐ _____
☐ _____
☐ _____
☐ _____
☐ _____
☐ _____
☐ _____

Projects to Start:

☐ _____
☐ _____
☐ _____
☐ _____
☐ _____
☐ _____
☐ _____
☐ _____
☐ _____
☐ _____

Monthly Blog Stats

# Of Unique Visits:	
# Of Overall Visits:	
Total Page Views	
Total Posts Made	
Total Comments	
Top 3 Popular Posts	
Top 3 Incoming Traffic Sources	
Top 3 Keyword Searches	

Goals for Next Month:

Projects to Finish:

- ☐ _____
- ☐ _____
- ☐ _____
- ☐ _____
- ☐ _____
- ☐ _____
- ☐ _____
- ☐ _____
- ☐ _____
- ☐ _____

Projects to Start:

- ☐ _____
- ☐ _____
- ☐ _____
- ☐ _____
- ☐ _____
- ☐ _____
- ☐ _____
- ☐ _____
- ☐ _____
- ☐ _____

Monthly Blog Stats

# Of Unique Visits:	
# Of Overall Visits:	
Total Page Views	
Total Posts Made	
Total Comments	
Top 3 Popular Posts	
Top 3 Incoming Traffic Sources	
Top 3 Keyword Searches	

Goals for Next Month:

Projects to Finish:

- ☐ _____
- ☐ _____
- ☐ _____
- ☐ _____
- ☐ _____
- ☐ _____
- ☐ _____
- ☐ _____
- ☐ _____
- ☐ _____

Projects to Start:

- ☐ _____
- ☐ _____
- ☐ _____
- ☐ _____
- ☐ _____
- ☐ _____
- ☐ _____
- ☐ _____
- ☐ _____
- ☐ _____

Monthly Blog Stats

# Of Unique Visits:	
# Of Overall Visits:	
Total Page Views	
Total Posts Made	
Total Comments	
Top 3 Popular Posts	
Top 3 Incoming Traffic Sources	
Top 3 Keyword Searches	

Goals for Next Month:

Projects to Finish:

- ☐ _____
- ☐ _____
- ☐ _____
- ☐ _____
- ☐ _____
- ☐ _____
- ☐ _____
- ☐ _____
- ☐ _____
- ☐ _____

Projects to Start:

- ☐ _____
- ☐ _____
- ☐ _____
- ☐ _____
- ☐ _____
- ☐ _____
- ☐ _____
- ☐ _____
- ☐ _____
- ☐ _____

Monthly Blog Stats

# Of Unique Visits:	
# Of Overall Visits:	
Total Page Views	
Total Posts Made	
Total Comments	
Top 3 Popular Posts	
Top 3 Incoming Traffic Sources	
Top 3 Keyword Searches	

Goals for Next Month:

Projects to Finish:

- ☐ _____
- ☐ _____
- ☐ _____
- ☐ _____
- ☐ _____
- ☐ _____
- ☐ _____
- ☐ _____
- ☐ _____
- ☐ _____

Projects to Start:

- ☐ _____
- ☐ _____
- ☐ _____
- ☐ _____
- ☐ _____
- ☐ _____
- ☐ _____
- ☐ _____
- ☐ _____
- ☐ _____

Monthly Blog Stats

# Of Unique Visits:	
# Of Overall Visits:	
Total Page Views	
Total Posts Made	
Total Comments	
Top 3 Popular Posts	
Top 3 Incoming Traffic Sources	
Top 3 Keyword Searches	

Goals for Next Month:

Projects to Finish:

- ☐ _____
- ☐ _____
- ☐ _____
- ☐ _____
- ☐ _____
- ☐ _____
- ☐ _____
- ☐ _____
- ☐ _____
- ☐ _____

Projects to Start:

- ☐ _____
- ☐ _____
- ☐ _____
- ☐ _____
- ☐ _____
- ☐ _____
- ☐ _____
- ☐ _____
- ☐ _____
- ☐ _____

Monthly Blog Stats

# Of Unique Visits:	
# Of Overall Visits:	
Total Page Views	
Total Posts Made	
Total Comments	
Top 3 Popular Posts	
Top 3 Incoming Traffic Sources	
Top 3 Keyword Searches	

Goals for Next Month:

Projects to Finish:

- ☐ _____
- ☐ _____
- ☐ _____
- ☐ _____
- ☐ _____
- ☐ _____
- ☐ _____
- ☐ _____
- ☐ _____
- ☐ _____

Projects to Start:

- ☐ _____
- ☐ _____
- ☐ _____
- ☐ _____
- ☐ _____
- ☐ _____
- ☐ _____
- ☐ _____
- ☐ _____
- ☐ _____

Monthly Blog Stats

# Of Unique Visits:	
# Of Overall Visits:	
Total Page Views	
Total Posts Made	
Total Comments	
Top 3 Popular Posts	
Top 3 Incoming Traffic Sources	
Top 3 Keyword Searches	

Goals for Next Month:

Projects to Finish:

- ☐ _____
- ☐ _____
- ☐ _____
- ☐ _____
- ☐ _____
- ☐ _____
- ☐ _____
- ☐ _____
- ☐ _____
- ☐ _____

Projects to Start:

- ☐ _____
- ☐ _____
- ☐ _____
- ☐ _____
- ☐ _____
- ☐ _____
- ☐ _____
- ☐ _____
- ☐ _____
- ☐ _____

Monthly Blog Stats

# Of Unique Visits:	
# Of Overall Visits:	
Total Page Views	
Total Posts Made	
Total Comments	
Top 3 Popular Posts	
Top 3 Incoming Traffic Sources	
Top 3 Keyword Searches	

Goals for Next Month:

Projects to Finish:

- ☐ _____
- ☐ _____
- ☐ _____
- ☐ _____
- ☐ _____
- ☐ _____
- ☐ _____
- ☐ _____
- ☐ _____
- ☐ _____

Projects to Start:

- ☐ _____
- ☐ _____
- ☐ _____
- ☐ _____
- ☐ _____
- ☐ _____
- ☐ _____
- ☐ _____
- ☐ _____
- ☐ _____

Thank you for purchasing this journal and using it for the need that you want.

I would appreciate any suggestions for improvement by writing it in your review of this product.

Go to Amazon find the journal and write your suggestion and reviews.

I have bought from Amazon one time and the inside of the book was crooked, so wrote to Kindle/Amazon about the problem. They corrected with a new paperback book.

I have seen many reviews where people get angry about the book being damage and they give a low ranking on the product. Remember the error is not the writer it is the printing from the publisher. So please don't take out your anger on the writer by giving them a low rating. Contact Amazon and request new book. Wait and then give review.

Awesome journal for keeping track of your computer log in, passwords, and website information.

The journal includes writing pages for keeping track of monthly goals or blogs.

The journal includes places for personal contacts and birthdates for the year.

This is the do all of journals for everyone.

www.ingramcontent.com/pod-product-compliance
Lightning Source LLC
Chambersburg PA
CBHW031248050326
40690CB00007B/1003